Loving God

LOVING GOD

Don't waste a moment. As soon you start meditating, reciting Nam, and seeking God's Light within yourself, your life will change. As more and more people do so, the world will change.

Baba Virsa Singh

BABA VIRSA SINGH

Loving God

The Practical Teachings

Baba Virsa Singh

A Sterling Paperback

STERLING PAPERBACKS
An imprint of
Sterling Publishers (P) Ltd.
A-59, Okhla Industrial Area, Phase-II,
New Delhi-110020.
Tel: 26387070, 26386209; Fax: 91-11-26383788
E-mail: sterlingpublishers@airtelbroadband.in
ghai@nde.vsnl.net.in
www.sterlingpublishers.com

Cover Photo: *Tatiana Batik*
Back Cover Photo: *Sergey Bermeniev*
Frontispiece: *Alexander Kucherenko*

Printed and Published by
Sterling Publishers Pvt. Ltd., New Delhi-110 020.

Contents

Baba Ji and His Work

Baba Virsa Singh ji is a holy person of Biblical proportions whose powerful spirituality was first recognized when he was a child. Born on 20 February 1934 in the rural village of Raja Jung outside of Lahore, he was uprooted in 1947 by Partition and moved with his family to Sarawan Bodla, a mud-brick village in Punjab, India. He spent his days plowing and working on the family farm, until one day in his late teens he experienced great anguish while cutting fodder for the animals. As the sap poured out, Babaji was consumed with the feeling that he had committed a great sin and prayed to be released from that duty. At once, sores appeared on the soles of his feet, so painful that he could not work. From that time, he began meditating day and night under the Beri tree in the courtyard, calling out to the One whose presence he could feel to "Please come – please show yourself." Babaji became so thin that his father took him to a local doctor. He still laughs when he remembers that time, as the doctor could not find anything wrong with him. Then one day, an awesome figure appeared to him. It was Baba Siri Chand ji, the great sixteenth-century mystic and elder son of Guru Nanak Dev ji, the first Sikh Guru. Not long thereafter, Baba Siri Chand ji returned and said, "I've brought my Father." There before the young man stood Guru Nanak Dev ji. Babaji recalls the scene as vividly as if it were today: "How can I ever forget the day? Of how He came and stood before me. Baba Siri Chand said 'I'll introduce you to my Father.' They were both very tall - over 6 feet. Guru Nanak Dev ji wore *lathu-wale karavan* (wooden sandals with a central "toe" knob) and his *chola* (long gown) was mouse-colored. He stood in front of me. I never bowed or anything. Baba Siri Chand ji, said 'My Father has come.' Guru Nanak spoke, 'So you think you need a Guru?' I said 'Yes.' 'Can you see my body?' I said, 'Yes'. 'Can you see my face?' I said yes. 'Do you see my lips moving? Repeat what I'm about to tell you and share it with others.' Then He said, 'Repeat after me – *Ek Onkar Satnam Siri WaheGuru* - recite this.' He gave me this shabad (sacred words) and said: 'Give this shabad to the people.' Then he said a very special thing. 'I received Nam this way myself.' That is a very profound thought. Then Guru Gobind Singh ji came. He had His own ways. He gave me many boons."

After that, Baba Siri Chand ji and Guru Gobind Singh ji were constantly with him, instructing the young man in strict meditation and in service to humanity. It was then that Baba Virsa Singh was shown that he would have to work very hard, that his fame and wealth would spread, that he would develop great farms, and perhaps most strange, that he would have a great following in Russia. When the boy began healing intractable diseases by giving people leaves from the Beri tree where he sat - or when the leaves were gone, simply by dipping his fingers in water - bringing the dead back to life, and transforming people's lives, villagers recognized that great spiritual powers were developing within him. They began to gather around him, and all have stories of the miracles that happened daily among his followers.

Obeying the command of God, Babaji moved from place to place, from Karnal in Haryana, North of Bareilly in UP, to Simla, Amritsar, Chandigarh and finally Delhi, reminding people of *dharam*, the Eternal Truths of all religions beyond any sectarian divisions. He was directed to some dry, thorny, rocky land at the south end of Delhi offered by a devotee Sardarni Nirlep Kaur. And in June of 1968 he began to develop that land into what is now Gobind Sadan, "God's House Without Walls"—a paradise of peaceful gardens, tree-lined paths, round-the-clock devotional centers, and a free community kitchen for people of all faiths and all social levels where miracles are everyday occurrences. He developed farms elsewhere as well, including the huge model farm known as Shiv Sadan, reclaimed from a dangerous flood-prone wasteland on the banks of the holy river Ganges.

People of all faiths and many countries come to Babaji at Gobind Sadan for his blessings and guidance, for practical spiritual training, for devotional worship, and for *seva* (voluntary service). Those working on the farms do strenuous manual labor from dawn to dusk, raising lush productive crops with yields far exceeding those in surrounding areas. The sevadars do not tire; they say they feel invigorated and blessed by the work. As they work, Babaji encourages them to silently recite God's Holy Name in loving remembrance *("Ik Onkar Sat Nam Siri Wahe Guru"—"There is One God whose name is Truth, Praise the Ever Greater, ever more wondrous God")*

The work supports Babaji¡'s mission to overcome poverty and religious conflict and bring peace to both individuals and the world. To heal those poor in spirit, prayers are offered round the clock. To uplift the deserving poor, langars (free community meals where people of all castes sit side by side on the ground), free medical care, schooling for children, are offered free of cost. And to teach reverence for all those who bring God's message and their teachings, Babaji holds interfaith gatherings and celebrates the major holidays of all religions.

Baba Virsa Singh makes no claim to being a guru; he does not seek fame, followers, or money. He says, "I am just trying to be a better human being. What I say is not new. I just repeat the commands of God so that people will remember them." The lives and teachings of the Sikh Gurus are the model for his practical work, yet he continually refers to the timeless teachings revealed by all Prophets. He stresses that sectarian divisions have been created by humans, not by God or God's Messengers. His basic program is the same for everyone: Recite Nam, read Jaap Sahib (Guru Gobind Singh's empowering Hymn of God's praises), do seva and rise early in the morning to begin thanking God and looking within yourself to battle with your own evils.

Babaji is highly respected as a world class leader, by scholars (though he has not received any formal worldly education), by government officials (though he seeks no one's favor), by scientists (who find

truth in Babaji's words and presence even
if they have been religious skeptics), and
by religious leaders and devotees of all
faiths (for he sincerely loves and
encourages appreciation of all Prophets
and scriptures). Although multitudes have
been blessed, healed and personally
transformed through his influence and by
following the practical program he
recommends, Babaji continually says, "God
is the only Doer, the One who gives you
everything. Give all your love to God."

The love of God is a basic theme
running through all of Babaji's teachings.
When he is not in secluded meditation, he
gives informal, spontaneous discourses. He
speaks in sweet and simple village Punjabi,
mixed with esoteric spiritual terms from
many languages and religions, charged
with profound spiritual meaning. These
discourses have inspired and transformed
the lives of countless people and have
produced practical demonstrations of God's
power to change the world. We have

gathered the essence of these teachings from many discourses and offer them to you topic by topic that you too may grow in your love for God.

One God

All religions are one. All the Prophets and Messiahs have repeatedly said that there is One God, whom we must love. No Prophet has said that there are two Truths or two Gods. There is One God, and we are to see Him in every planet and person, in animals, oceans, mountains. But we will only be able to see God in all of His Creation when the love of God emerges within us.

God is the Power that runs everything. When saints or Prophets have seen or heard this Power through *gyan*, the divine wisdom of enlightenment, they then spoke of that Power in words that became the Divine Names for God. All are referring to the same One.

One enlightened person saw that there is One Power giving light to everyone. He said, "Ik Onkar" (You are One). Another saw that Power controlling all the waters— waves, rivers, oceans of water. He called that Controller "Narayan" (the One who is present in water).

Another person saw that One Light is giving life to everything. When he looked within himself, he found the same light there. He said, "Sohang" which means "Whatever You are, so too am I." Another person saw that God's Light is everywhere: "You are in Darkness as well as in Light." He referred to this Power as "Gobind" (Remover of darkness and Bringer of light). Another person who saw this Power found it so wondrous that he had no words for it. All he could say was "Wah!"(Wonderful!). Still another saw that Power is infinite, beyond description. He said, "Neti, neti, neti" (beyond, beyond, beyond).

Such descriptions from an enlightened state are not contradictory. They are all describing the same Power, whether in Sanskrit, Arabic, Punjabi, Urdu, Latin or English. There are differences in the words, but not in the Being.

God is one Light. It comes in the person who meditates and who is filled with love. Only this person can perceive the Power. First look within yourself, and then you will see God everywhere.

Prophets of One Light

God has been here from the beginning; God will go on forever. But from time to time, the number of people who have pure minds full of faith in and love for God decreases. The people have forgotten; their minds have become impure and they do not listen to a Power they cannot see. Then God, who is both manifest and un-manifest, has to come in the physical form of a Prophet. For people will only follow someone whom they can see and hear. With God's blessings, God's grace, and God's mercy, this person begins to realize

God, and God's Power and Light start working through his tongue and heart.

God chooses Prophets but does not reveal anything to them in the beginning. When the right time comes, God gives them gyan. God then discloses certain things to them at certain times, but still keeps many things secret. After God begins using a person as His Messenger, that person no longer works from his own mind or his own heart. It is all God's work.

All the Prophets have come from the same light; they all give the same basic messages. None have come to change the older revealed scriptures; they have come to remind people of the earlier Prophets' messages which the people have forgotten. We have made our separate religions into walled forts, each claiming one of the Prophets as its own. But the Light of God cannot be confined within any manmade structures. It radiates throughout all of creation. How can we possess it?

None of the Prophets belongs to just one caste, one creed, or one nation. Jesus is not confined to Christianity; Moses is not a Jew; the Prophet Mohammad is not a Muslim; Guru Nanak is not a Sikh. They have not come to establish institutionalized, sectarian religions. Those divisions are created by humans and reflect their own policies. By contrast, the Prophets come into the world with a message from God. They come to remind people of God's teachings, making them fresh and new again; they come to teach love, to encourage service to humanity, to remove ignorance by enlightening people with the knowledge of God. They come to change our consciousness; they come to show us how to live.

Human beings do have spiritual wisdom deep within themselves; the One who creates the world is already sitting in their souls. But it is only when a Prophet of God comes down and starts speaking with Divine Wisdom that it awakens in people. The Prophet reminds them of the truth they know but have forgotten.

Dharam

Dharam is our universal term for God's Divine Laws, which govern and empower everything from human behavior and worship to the movements of the universe. It is beyond dogma and sects. Sectarian religions have been made by humans, not by the Prophets. The truly spiritual person is above all these small paths. God is nearer than your hands and feet, sitting in your heart, bringing more and more light inside you. God does not need any more praise from us; the whole universe is already praising God. God is so famous that He is concealing Himself. But even though we can add nothing to God's greatness by our praise, we must ever remember God through love, faith and service.

Dharam is not costly temples. It is not the light of a single Prophet; God's Messengers continually come into the world to show people the way. It is not a particular concept of God, for nothing is outside of God.

Religion must never be used to further our own purposes or power. Religion is God's Love. Jesus told his disciples, "Just as I share this love freely with you, share that love freely with everyone. Never think to profit from it. You should have no demands, just as I make no demands of you."

Dharam is not theory; it is practical application. Whenever dharam has spread in the world, it has given practical proof of its truth. The Prophets have not just described trees and flowers; they have produced them and shown their beauty to the people. People have very little faith in religion because today there is only talk. For spiritual teachers as well as devotees, putting the teachings into practice requires a life of meditation and love for the Creator. Each religion has two aspects: vision and history. Vision is spiritual. It is born of the inner light, of the Spirit. The all-pervading Light of God is seen through the inner light of gyan in a person, and the words born out of that Light are visionary revelations. Those words can only be understood when we meditate and search within ourselves for God's Light, the source of that vision.

Dharam has no connection with that aspect of a religion that comes from those who just want to prove their own intelligence, and not from the Prophets. History also includes rituals and restrictions on behavior that develop after the visionary basis of the religion. The Prophet Mohammad, in his greatness and his humility said, *"If sometimes you do not follow the Hadith,* (reports of what the Prophet Mohammad said, did, or approved), *God will forgive you. But if you do not follow what is revealed in the Quran, God will not pardon you."*

Most of what we call religion today is simply management, not vision. It is based on selfish motives. Where there is selfishness, there is no dharam.

It is our limited thinking that has created the forts and slogans of religions. If you approach the scriptures of all religions from a state of inner wisdom, you will find many similarities among them. What is the essence of religion? Truthfulness, love, faith in God, and service to everyone. We should transcend these sectarian barriers, think of each other as fellow human beings, and regard all Prophets as our Fathers. They all came to love us.

Science and Dharam

Dharam is the greatest science. Hundreds and in some cases thousands of years ago, visionaries revealed to us what scientists are just now heralding as their latest discovery. The visionaries simply closed their eyes, sat comfortably in meditation, and described what they saw. They did not have to spend huge sums on research or waste battery cell power. We human beings have many powerful brain cells. Once they are developed through meditation we can observe the entire universe – from the microscopic to the vast expanse of the cosmos.

What is meditation? concentrating on something, researching it, looking deeply into it, until you reach a conclusion. Whether you are conducting scientific research or meditating and having visions, both are a matter of inner concentration.

The stronger and clearer your mind, and the more you are able to focus your thoughts, the better scientist you will become. Likewise, the clearer your mind and the greater your power of concentration, the better saint you will become. Worry, fear, and pressure should not enter, for they will torture your mind. In reality, meditation is our mind's defense. It keeps out the bad and develops the good.

Actually, scientists are only proving what has already been revealed. Our country's ancient religious texts had already told us that some stars are so far away that it will take tens of millions of years for their rays to reach the earth. Five hundred years ago, while in meditation, Guru Nanak once said, "This sun you see is not the only sun—there are tens of millions of suns. This moon is not the only moon—there are tens of millions of such bodies." When you see that celestial drama, you begin to think about this earthly drama in which we live. This is just a tiny speck in the vastness of the cosmos.

Sometimes a scientist becomes worried when the parts of his research do not fit together. At that point, he needs the help of an enlightened one to share his store of knowledge and clear the obstruction in the scientist's mind. Then his research can move ahead. The scientist knows about the elements, but sometimes they may confuse him. Inner spiritual knowledge will never confuse a person.

Unfortunately, though the fields of the scientist and the saint are related, they never collaborate. The scientist feels, "I am so learned, why should I sit with an illiterate person?" For his part, the saint feels, "The scientist is an atheist. What have I to do with him?" Where there is dharam, oceans and oceans of knowledge have coalesced. It is our misfortune that we have not been able to explain dharam in a way that scientists could understand.

Both the scientist and the saint are studying the universe. The scientist studies its components; the saint studies the One who made them. But both conclude that no matter how much they have discovered, there is still endless vastness beyond. When the scientist and the saint ultimately sit together, the knowledge of the universe will increase, and humanity will benefit greatly. Then the scientist will start believing in God; the saint already does so.

Realizing God

The outward form of religion is bowing your head before God in a church, temple, or mosque. But until your mind and spirit bow in humility to God, spiritual progress is not possible. The physical body is only the house of our spirit. When our spirit is awakened, the confidence, faith, love and willingness to serve which will arise within us will be so powerful that we ourselves will be unable to understand the changes that come over us.

Look to the One who gives birth to all religions. Don't think that God is a theory;

God is reality. If you think God is a theory, you will never become enlightened. And don't think that you can ever be separated from God. As the Guru Granth Sahib (Sikh scripture) says, *"God is sitting inside you, nearer than your hands and feet. The distance between you and God is as thin as a butterfly's wing. We can never be separated from God—neither at birth nor at death."* Nor do our mistakes separate us from God. God is always forgiving.

God does not say, "I want you to surrender before me." God says, "I do not want you to be slaves. I have made you free." But negative things are attracted to our mind and stick there, forming a curtain between us and God. If we simply think of surrendering our negative points, they will become slightly detached. As soon as one side is detached, the whole curtain falls away, revealing the light of gyan. Gyan is always inside us, hidden by the curtain of ignorant ego-centered thoughts. This curtain is not like stone. It is quite thin, has no weight, and can be broken very easily, just by a mere thought of surrendering.

To be aware of the presence of God, you must clean your mind and be grateful to the One who is the only Giver, the only Doer. Think that everything in this world exists with God's blessing, whether we regard it as pleasant or unpleasant. Only God knows what is good for us.

If God's love is in your mind, you will see that nothing in the world is without this Love. When you love God, you will start seeing Him among the animals, the trees, the inanimate things. God is present even in that which we cannot see. Only the one who is absorbed in God recognizes His presence. Such a person has given her mind to God, and thus attained God. There is so much love in God that all the rivers— the whole universe—can be filled with it. The moment you touch God, you become filled with love. That Light will not be

found in any worldly religious show or
building.

That Light lives in our mind, in the
mind filled with love. Wherever we are
sitting—in the forests, fields, or
mountains—God gives light to the loving
mind.

God is waiting at the gate. But no one
is standing in line. All the gates are empty.
No one is waiting there to enter. So let us
pass through that gate where love dwells,
and only love.

Meditation

Meditation is a magnificent power. With meditation, you gain the desire to serve and the ability to achieve your spiritual and worldly goals; you develop compassion, fearlessness, divine wisdom, renunciation, love, and freedom from the cycle of births and deaths. Meditation allows us to meet with the King of our spirit.

To meditate is to become deeply silent, to keep listening, listening, listening to God. To listen is to become lost in God,

34

perceiving Him in all of creation. Then one is merged with the Great Reality. No worldly pleasure can compare with the sweetness of this communion.

There are many yogic postures and methods of meditation, but even by practicing them you cannot attain God unless you feel the longing of love. God is Love, and God is too great for any method. It is God who pulls us to meditate, and it is God who teaches us how to love Him.

The only method of meditation that works is to offer God constant love. At first, continually focus all your scattered attention on whatever form of God you worship—your *Isht*, such as Lord Jesus, Lord Krishna, Lord Siva, Durga Mata, or the Gurus. And because it is the nature of the mind to wander, we can concentrate on God by repeating God's Name. The energy which has been scattered among all our weaknesses will become focused on the positive; negative thoughts will disappear and truth will be revealed in our mind.

The more we meditate, bringing our attention back again and again, the sooner it will return to its Home. Once it comes back Home, it will listen and it will rest. Then there will be only peace. Start this way, and then God will show you the path. Make no demands, except for one: "Oh God, make me as You want me to be."

Early in the morning, when you first arise, thank God and do a little bit of meditation. Go deep inside, concentrating all your awareness on God. Then the whole day your mind will be focused on God; nothing will bother you. The more you love God and practice meditation, your weaknesses and bad habits will be driven out, and love and truth will be revealed, as if dust were being cleaned from a mirror.

In deep meditation, your awareness of yourself ceases. You are unaware of the passing time, and you do not become tired. Your breathing becomes fainter. People may be beating drums or shouting around you, but you will not hear anything. Your soul rises above your body; it maintains just enough connection to keep you alive.

Over time, very gradually, the inner light, divine wisdom, vision, and truth will awaken in you. Your Isht will enter your heart and start loving and talking to you. As the Sikh Gurus say, *"Sometimes you laugh, sometimes you cry, and sometimes you become silent, but you care for no one except God."* You will become detached from worldly things, for you are always connected with the Truth. You will not care if people are looking at you or laughing at you for you are looking only at God, absorbed in the bliss of God's Love.

As you continually look toward God, your state of mind will keep changing. Eventually your Isht will disappear, and you will see only God everywhere. You will recognize that everything is happening according to God's orders. God will speak to you in the form of Light and be visible everywhere as Light.

Then you will not need to sit in meditation with your eyes closed in order to be aware of God. You will be joined with God at all times. Whether you are walking, eating, or talking to someone. You will truly feel, *"Tohi mohi, mohi Tohi"* (You are me, and I am You). You will remain in the world, doing your worldly duties, and you will be always happy.

Nam

Nam (God's Holy Name) is like an ocean. Service and charity but streams. We are seeking something small, but with the help of Nam, oceans of priceless jewels await us.

Reciting Nam is a way of thanking and praising the Nami—the omnipresent, timeless Creator. It is a path to God for everybody. When you recite Nam and love God without any motives, He will cleanse your mind, there will be great light in your heart, and your whole family will be blessed. Nam will heal your mind, eliminating all negative thoughts; only positive thoughts will remain. The hidden joy and love and fearlessness within you will become manifest.

Actually, it is not that God wants our praises. The effect of Nam works on us. Our body is just a house where we live. Our life is governed by our karmas—the effects on our life of our sanskars, our habitual thoughts and actions from this life and from previous births. Our karmas are like great waves that are not under our control. Nam breaks those waves.

As we recite Nam—with our tongue, with our mind, with every breath—those waves start to break up here and there. You may be worrying as usual—"What will happen?"—but as you recite Nam there is a small break in that train of thought. You feel, "It will be okay." But at this stage you are still reciting Nam only with your tongue. Your thoughts and awareness are not on Nam, and soon your mind returns to its old patterns.

As you go on reciting Nam, you will experience a little light inside, a brief moment of *samadhi* (spiritual absorption). But then the mind starts running away again at great speed, and the little bit of light disappears. Then longing for God may begin to grow in you, although it is very faint at first. As you are singing or reciting Nam, you may experience a brief communion with the Nami.

To become closer to God, you should focus your mind on your *Isht*, that form of God in whom you have faith. At first, your Isht may seem just a faint image in your mind, but gradually its presence becomes a reality. Slowly that Power gives your mind confidence and you begin loving that Isht you are trying to focus your attention on. It takes a long time, but gradually you will feel the presence of your Isht within you.

Once you feel your Isht inside you, through the power of Nam, you will begin to see that your Isht is actually controlling everything outside you as well. You will see your Isht pervading everywhere and everything.

As you keep reciting Nam, whenever you begin to feel anger, greed, or ego the feeling does not last long. It moves aside. Why? Nam is washing away the dirt of your past tendencies; the Light of divine wisdom is burning up your past actions. Gradually, you cease to feel anger or greed, and you feel that you are nothing great. You become very humble.

All ignorance ceases as the light of Nam manifests fully. If you reach this stage of enlightenment through continual recitation of Nam and concentration on the Nami, you will see only God everywhere. Like God, you will feel neither enmity nor fear. You will recognize that the Nami is sustaining and controlling all life. Nam will make your actions bright and will give you clear inner vision, truthfulness, renunciation, the desire to help those in need, and the power to do anything, for the Power of the Nami has manifested in you.

Worship

Why is there no spiritual attainment in religion today? We perform our own kind of rituals, but we do not worship with love. Instead, we look at our watches and see that we have spent five or ten minutes. We do not concentrate on worship. Perhaps we have placed flowers, bathed the statue with milk, lit some incense, bowed our head, and our mind is satisfied. But this satisfaction is false. These actions are all right, but they will not change our fate.

When we stand before our worldly
father, we bow and ask, "Father, what are
your orders?" He gives us some work, and
we are to do that. When we go to a religious
place, our Heavenly Father also gives us
orders. He says, *"My child, always tell the
truth. Do not steal. It is wrong to criticize
others. Do not deprive others of their rights.
Do unto others as you would have them do
unto you. Do not covet what is your
neighbor's."* We may have gone to our
Heavenly Father every day, offered flowers
to Him, bathed a statue with milk,
worshipped Him for ten minutes, but we
have not obeyed a single commandment.
It is amazing: We sit before Him every day
but we still only do what comes to our own
mind. We do not even come close to
following what He says.

We should be keenly aware that a place
of worship is a school for the mind, a school
for cleansing the impurities from our mind.
But how do we behave in this school? We
take the first primer in our hands but we

do not read it. We bow our head and make some demands, but we do not obey the commandments. This means that we have been holding the same primer for many years, but we have never even once read it. How can we advance to the second book? The second book will only be given to us after we have obeyed the commandments in the first book.

In worldly terms, after a person studies, eventually he attains something. After twenty-five or thirty-five years, he passes his subjects and completes the course, and thereafter receives some employment. Why is there no such attainment in religion? Because we truly think that a religious school is only a place to bow our heads, and that by bowing we can achieve everything. But let me stress that there is no school anywhere in which we can attain anything by just bowing our heads. One can achieve something only through action.

Look at history: With whom was God pleased? To whom did God speak? To those who deeply loved God with open hearts. They saw God in the trees, in the land, in the skies. God spoke to them.

When we go to religious places, we offer cash to the religious authorities who say, "We will pray to God for you." But I don't think He wants our money. God is not poor. God is not a beggar. God is so powerful that He is distributing wealth to the whole Creation. He gives us breath, energy, clothing, employment, the very bed on which we sleep. He is such a great Giver that His bounty has no limits. When a priest expects something from people and begs, it is a great insult to God, for he turns God into a beggar in the public's eyes.

God is not a beggar. God is the Giver. God is always distributing Light, distributing blessing. Simply offering money is not acceptable to God. Instead, the Gurus says, *"God is hungry for love and devotion."* God says, *"Please come to Me*

*with love, and fill yourself with My Love.
If you can pay the fees of a poor student,
use the cash in that way. If there is a widow
in need, help her. If a person cannot
purchase medicines, use this money to help
him."*

It is just possible that we have not
achieved enlightenment because we have
turned such a great Giver into a pauper.
We just throw cash in front of Him, but
He doesn't want it. We offer a little money
and say, "I have done this, I have given
this," but what can we do? This mind is
His, this body is His, and this wealth is
also His. What can we give to Him? The
Gurus say, *"Give your mind, body, and
wealth to Him and obey His
commandments, and only then will you
attain something."*

When we are full of love, then we
worship from our heart. When the saint
Nam Dev was a boy, his father instructed
him to offer milk daily to the statue in their
home while he was away. Innocent Nam

Dev did not know that his father always drank the milk himself after offering it to the statue. So when Nam Dev offered the milk and the statue did not take it, he begged, "Please drink this offering, my Lord." The statue still did not drink the milk. Nam Dev persisted, "Do you want us to have a fight in our family? If you do not drink this milk, my father will be very angry with me." He kept pleading with the statue. Finally, the hand reached out from the statue and drank all the milk. The father had been performing this ritual for years but had attained nothing. But when Nam Dev approached the statue innocently, in love, the Lord started drinking milk and speaking to him from the statue, because God is in every place.

We sit before God but we do not understand that we have to talk to Him. We just do our duty. We take some flowers, some little things, and after two minutes bow our head and go home. God must surely be laughing, *"It is amazing! They*

*must think I am just a formality. They do
not obey even one of my teachings, and yet
every day they ritually bow before me and
then make a lot of demands. They serve
little and demand much."*

It is good to worship. But worship from
the heart. If we stand before an image of a
manifestation of God, we should use it to
focus our scattered mind, to concentrate
our attention on God. Eventually, the
image will begin to move, to speak. Then
that One will begin sitting inside us. When
it lives within us, it becomes Light, and
nothing else is left except Light. Then we
will talk to the trees and the animals. God
will speak to us from within our own mind,
because it has become pure. The real
temple of God is a pure mind.

Mental Freedom

We think we are free, but freedom does not mean we can do all sorts of bad things without any consequences. A person who lives that way is bound, a slave to his raving mind and passions. Freedom means not being a slave to any habit. We are so bound by our bad habits that we cannot escape them. We live in our own egos. The Gurus say, *"Where there is I-centeredness, God is not there. When God comes, the ego vanishes."* In thinking, "This is mine, I am this," we create many difficulties in our lives. By contrast, when our ego is gone, God takes care of us and brings us success. As Guru Gobind Singh says, *"The One who is the Remover of Difficulties comes and stands before you."*

Meditation is essential to develop will power. When your thoughts are under control, you become free. When your mind is clear, you can conquer the whole world.

As the Prophet Mohammad says, *"Do jihad"*—struggle for good. The greatest jihad, he says, is to control the raving mind. Guru Nanak likewise said to struggle against your weaknesses — by rising in the early morning ambrosial hours to meditate and by working hard all day or night.

Your mind is like a horse. If your horse is strong, it will outdistance all the other horses. If it is weak, no matter how much you urge it on, it fails. If it is untamed, it may throw you. Today, all the horses are out of control. Like a horse who keeps throwing its rider, our thoughts are shaking us from within. "What is going to happen now? Things are not going according to my plans." Everyone's mind is out of control, so accidents happen—we hurt each other's feelings, take away other's rights, and attack others. All the horses are wild and untamed. No rider is able to hold onto the reins. How can you rein in your wild horse? Control your desires. You need not even use your own strength. Rather, start loving God and meditating. It is best if the reins are in God's hands. Know that whatever God does is right.

In addition, always try to live close to nature, for you will be very near to God. Worry, fear, and pressure will be far from you. Your mind will be open, free, and clear, with no enmity. Your mind will be fearless, kind, and full of love. The muscles of your mind—as well as of your body—will be strong. A person with a strong mind is not susceptible to evil; it cannot enter his thoughts. His mind goes straight ahead. And one day his inner truth mixes with the Great Truth.

Faith and Surrender

We say, "Oh God, everything is yours." But we are only speaking with our tongue, not with our heart. God knows our inner self. When we truly offer everything to God, He gives us everything to use, though not to own. To feel that Someone Else is the owner of these things frees us.

Guru Arjan Dev says, *"Whosoever has God as his friend never wants for anything."* He has all happiness, he has all joy, because his dealings are with God. Whatever he says will be fulfilled by his Father.

We need not worry. The only thing we should worry about is whether we have hurt anyone's feelings or deprived anyone of their rights. It is God's job to take care of us, just as God takes care of all creatures.

God has given us a mind that is so tender, so full of love and truth. But we harden it by worrying. From morning to evening, we worry about what will happen next. Our anxiety actually creates accidents. Instead, hold fast to truth, love, and joy by loving God. We should at last admit that nothing happens without God's orders. We should unite with the One who gives the orders.

Jesus was asked, "Master, what are you? At your word, the fig tree which was not bearing fruit has withered, the wind has stopped, the waves of the ocean have subsided, and the water has become like a road beneath your feet. What are you?" Jesus replied, *"I am nothing. The difference between you and me is that I have faith. I know that everything is under my Father's command. When I see my Father and say something, my father immediately does that. If you have faith even the size of a mustard seed, your thought can move a mountain."*

We should pray, "Dear God, please give us that faith which cleans our mind of all doubts, leaving only love." Once you receive God's love, you will be filled with so much love for Him that whatever you ask of God, He will provide.

Even if you do good deeds and follow a spiritual discipline, you still may experience difficulties in the world. But do not lose faith, for through these difficulties, the actions of your past lives are being cleared away. People assume that everything should go according to their own desires. That cannot be. Our lives are shaped by our past deeds and thoughts, from hundreds of thousands of previous lives. Our karmas from all these lives form a crust of filth on our mind. If we want to change our fortune we must burn our karmas with the fire of meditation. Sometimes so much rubbish has accumulated that even if we set it on fire it will keep burning for days. With such heaps of rubbish, it is unrealistic to think that we will achieve something simply by performing some special worship for ten days or forty days. Trying to bargain with God like this is of no value. Whether we worship God or not does not add to or detract from His greatness. The whole of Creation is already worshipping Him. Where we crave results there are desires. And where there are desires, there is no true love of God. Think, "Whatever I have done, I have received my due." Do not blame others for what happens to you.

It is the person who has cleared all his karmas who knows God as the One who fulfills all desires and gives all happiness—*Icha purakh, Sarab Sukh Data*. There is no difference between him and God, between his thought and the thought of God.

In order to be made into precious jewelry, gold must first be melted in the furnace. A washer-man whacks and whacks clothes to clean them. It is not that God treats us unkindly; we are drubbed to cleanse our filth and to purify our mind. The filth will only leave us through constant pounding. pounding, pounding.

God says, *"I am the Doer of whatever is happening. Accept this. Don't worry, don't become angry or envious. You know only one birth, but your age is actually hundreds of thousands of years. These things only appear to be difficulties because you do not understand them. Think of them instead as My Love. Actually, the sword was coming to cut off your head, but only its shadow has brushed you."*

Jesus said, *"Anyone who walks toward me and faces difficulties along the way is blessed. If they are coming to me and other people trouble them, they are blessed; if they become sick, if they are poor, if people are stoning them as they walk toward me, they are blessed."*

Many infants were killed by the king when Jesus was born. The king had learned that a great power had been born and he hoped to end that threat to his supremacy by ordering all the babies in the area killed. Many babies were killed, but Jesus's parents took him away safely. As soon as the king passed that order, God ordered that the new Sun should rise quickly, and the king's light was covered with darkness. God embraced Jesus and kissed him, and said, *"My son, whatever I say to you will remain forever on the earth."* The infants who died for the sake of Jesus were all reborn into great houses; they enjoyed worldly blessings and they themselves became great. People who are killed for the sake of a Prophet of God are always reborn into very good lives; they are especially blessed by God. God is very watchful when His Prophets come to the world. It is a period of great blessings.

Death

The soul never dies. But when we look at it from our limited human standpoint, we think, "He was an old man; it was his time to go. But why did the young person have to die?" There is a great secret behind this. Though a person may appear to be a child to us, if we were able to look within them, we would see that his soul is not that of a child. He has already taken many births. He has left the world and returned many times.

Dharam continually teaches us that there is no such thing as death, even

60

though all things leave the world. So why is it so difficult for us to accept? Human nature is very loving. We humans never forget anything which leaves us. Even if the cup breaks from which we drank our tea every day, we will remember it for many days. Why? Because we loved that cup. When the family dog dies, we don't eat for days. When our love for another person is so much greater, it is naturally very difficult to forget them. It is especially difficult to accept the death of a person whose heart was filled with kindness and love, who always thought about others, and was always concerned that others should not suffer. But people cannot fully understand God's rules.

When a child dies, to us it is a tragic event. But God is like a farmer who decides when the time has come to harvest his crop. The Guru has said, *"Sometimes He cuts His crop before it has ripened, sometimes He waits until it is half-grown, and sometimes He waits until it is ripe."*

LOVING GOD

We say, "We want to see that form, we want to hear that voice." But the one we love is going to take birth again. Their innocence, their power, their karma will be reborn. We should never forget that all the Prophets called this world *mirt lok*— "the transient world"—for nothing here remains. The body will definitely leave some day. Lord Krishna said, *"What is death? You simply exchange your old clothes for new ones. There is no death for us."* But the nature of life, death, and karma is a subject for the Prophets. The average person has difficulty understanding it.

No doubt, we are filled with sorrow when a loved one dies. But we should not be annoyed with God or ask "Why did this happen?", because the person was carrying his karma from previous lives. Remember also that even while people are crying here, somewhere else people are offering congratulations as he is reborn. They are rejoicing, "A good child has come to our house at last." He has gone on to be born in a home where he was greatly needed. And although his body has gone from this life, his thoughts will never leave. If they were good thoughts, people will continue to benefit from them.

We should therefore pray that God will send our loved one to a good place, where he can continue his good work and continue to develop his or her thoughts. Dharam teaches us that progress does not occur in just one lifetime. For example, a person does not become a good doctor in one lifetime. She has studied the body many times, and after many births, she becomes familiar with each part of the body. A scientist has been pursuing his research for many lifetimes. At one point, he realizes the essence of his research and develops something. Some children at the age of three or five start creating buildings or taking photographs, because these are the things they were doing in their past lives. The child picks up from where he left off.

We have been here many times before and left many times, but we do not know it. It is a secret that God has kept hidden from us.

Healing

Wherever God is remembered night and day, such a blessed atmosphere will be created that healing occurs automatically. However, the greatest healing comes from looking to see what lies within ourselves. We all have a wonderful power within us. Whether we are poor or rich, sinner or saint, we all have Light within us. The greatest truth that comes from going deep inside our self is that we recognize that Power which lies within us as Light. When we are in love with God, kindness and love and the desire to serve others will develop within us. When our mind is healed, our thoughts will become very pure and holy, and our body will also be very happy.

By contrast, fear, hatred, anger, and egotism have very negative effects on the body. This is our greatest ailment—that we have fear, hatred, ego, and anger within us. Whenever we are under the influence of anger, every part of our body trembles. When we are afraid, fear weakens our mind and also our body. The disease of nervousness, of worry, afflicts ninety percent of people. If this affliction is eradicated from the mind, all physical diseases will also end.

We may try to heal our body with the help of herbs, or allopathic medicine, or homeopathy. But who will heal our thoughts? The body may of course be healed and the ailment eliminated. But it is our thoughts that irritate us.

Throughout the world, people are trying to find comfort by every means possible, be it yoga or medicine or acquiring big cars and big houses. Despite all this, people are not happy. We should instead transform our mind, our thoughts. When we heal our mind, disease will have little chance to enter our body, and negative thoughts will not have the opportunity to pollute our mind.

Humans are the most poisonous of all creatures. When we become angry and commit a crime, a wave of poison spreads through the atmosphere. If we purify our thoughts, if we make them loving, serving, and compassionate, I think the environment of the whole world will be cleansed.

When our thoughts are poisoning us, how will worldly medicine help us? If we could achieve pleasure through medicine, then those rulers with very learned doctors would be supremely happy. But both the rulers and the doctors are unhappy.

The medicine for our thoughts is not worldly medicine. We can get it only from

LOVING GOD

meditation. When we turn within and meet God, we will all be healed. God will heal our inner sickness and our outer sickness as well.

Seva

Guru Nanak introduced a new path to spiritual attainment. He said, *"Let me show you the direct path to God: Work hard to support yourself by honest means, always remember God, and share the fruits of your labors for the uplift of humanity."* Nam (reciting God's Holy Name) without seva (voluntary work in service to God's Creation) is not acceptable to Guru Nanak: *"If people retreat to the mountains to recite Nam, who will put out the fires of the burning world?"* Every person has to work and help others, for this is God's *hukam* (divine command). One who simply sits idle and meditates will not find favor in God's court, and because he is not helping people, he will not find favor in the world either.

God is the greatest Worker. He is always busy caring for everything – the trees, the people, the earth. If God is constantly working in the world, then how can those who say they believe in God sit idle? Those who become part of this mission tend to work four times harder than anyone else. The power that comes from their love of God not only brings out that work ethic but also the strength to follow it. Work with your hands and feet and keep your mind joined with God. Work is a form of meditation if your mind is in a state of love. If your mind is attuned with dedication, you are with the Creator as you are serving. If your mind is far away – if you are thinking of your family or friends for instance – then you are not able to do the dedicated work you are supposed to do.

When you combine work and worship, you can work harder and serve more.

God works so hard and is always happy. If we love God, we will be happy while we are serving and we will always remain with Him.

Mission

The main thing is to be involved in a positive program – a mission. A mission is a program made by God; it is guided by God's *hukam*. Whether you are sleeping, standing, or thinking, the mission should be in your thoughts. If a person is committed to a mission, even if something happens in his family he will not be concerned. His mind is still firmly engaged in the mission. Even if he must lay down his life for his mission, he will not be afraid. He is so whole-heartedly committed to the program that it *is* his life; in fulfilling his mission he does not feel that he is sacrificing anything. He will praise God for being so kind to allow him to accomplish His mission. He feels, "May all my lifetimes be devoted to this mission. Even if I have forty more lives, I will continue to work for this mission. Nothing must enter this program that will damage our goal."

Everyone has goals, but most people have the wrong goals, such as sleeping, drinking, and producing children. People with these goals are not much different from animals. Human goals should be beneficial, such as doing seva and helping society.

How can we develop the motivation to serve? By meditating. And how can we develop the desire to meditate? By starting to meditate and depending on God. I have no personal mission. I simply work to put forth God's message that has already been given to others: We are to serve the poor and work to uplift humanity. I have full faith that if people of all religions come

together and work in service to humanity,
the whole world can come together in
harmony. But we must set aside our self-
interest and work in selfless service to
others. We must be so strict in our program
that God will always take care of us, just
as a father runs to help his child at all
times.

Overcoming Poverty

Poverty is not a permanent state. There is no such class or nation we can call "the poor." Work hard and thank God and He will lift you out of poverty. That is my personal experience. The policies of the world are wrong – there should be no poverty.

The basic goal of all religions is to take those things that are not in productive use—be they land, trees, or the human mind—and help them develop. As part of God's commitment to the Prophets, God has always commanded them, *"Go and prosper, and make these minds and lands productive.*" Adam planted wheat; Noah planted grapes; Guru Nanak cultivated the soil with his own hands. God commanded them to make the land productive. This commandment from God continues today. Food is needed for people's bodies, just as Nam is needed as food for the mind.

Jesus said he would find the lambs who were lagging behind and reunite them with the flock; he would lift the lambs that were lost and carry them to the herd. He was referring to his great love for those who have been rejected by society: "*I have come for you. You are not going to be lost now.*"

Religion does not lie in erecting big edifices as houses for God. God does not have time to sit there being worshipped. Rather, God is here in the world, constantly working with the poor and needy, for the uplift of humanity.

When we erect an elaborate religious building, it simply increases the burden on people and diverts resources from the

76

alleviation of poverty. Instead, if we take barren land and develop it, sow crops there, we can use that income to decrease poverty and help the poor to rise. Our program is to take all of nature that is lying waste, not being used properly, and help reclaim it, for the benefit of all people, regardless of their nationality, creed, or race. Those who love God should always be thinking about what problems exist in their particular areas, and spend their time working to alleviate those problems.

As Guru Amar Das prayed, *"Oh God, the whole world is on fire."* People are suffering in sorrow and oppression; the environment is suffering. The Guru prayed, *"Please bless and relieve the suffering of the entire creation. From whatever path people approach You, please bless them."*

I have full faith that if those who preach the word of God would all get involved and begin to work productively again—rather than just sitting idle and taking money for themselves and for big buildings in God's name—we would be able to overcome many of the current difficulties in the world.

We should all work hard and serve humanity, but keep ourselves out of the picture. We should constantly thank God as the only Doer: *"Dear Lord, this work that I have done is all Your work. I have done nothing. This is all Your grace."* To love God is not to sit idle and say, "Oh God, You are responsible for everything." Rather, we should work incredibly hard to overcome the difficulties in the world. We should meet every adversity and then pray, *"Dear Lord, this service and this success are all due to Your grace. I have done nothing."*

As one meditates, one becomes aware of everyone's needs and is always concerned for their well-being. One cares for the poor who work all day but still cannot meet their basic needs. Guru Amar Das has said, *"Worry about others."* One continually prays, "Please God, give them food, give them clothing, please make their life easier. And in addition to their physical sustenance, please give them spiritual sustenance too."

Make God Your Friend

Guru Granth Sahib says, *"The one whose Friend is God can never be separated from God. He will never come nor go from the presence of the Indestructible One."* God is always present with us, nearer than our hands and feet.

Why should we abandon such a House where caste and lineage do not matter, where there is no high or low? God always receives everyone, saying, "Welcome! Come!" He is always forgiving, always merciful. As Guru Gobind Singh says, *"He does not point out our drawbacks."* Guru Nanak says, *"You are my Mother, You are my Father, You are my dearest Friend."* Make God your Friend and then see what He will do: He will throw open the gates of blessings.

Peace of mind is not dependent on one's surroundings. When you love someone their presence fills your thoughts at all times. When you love God, then God is with you at all times and the peace you receive is indescribable. There is no greater peace than that which results from this love.

Once Guru Gobind Singh, in a very loving mood said, *"Listen very carefully: Only those who truly love God can ever find Him."* This is the essential inner secret.

The Coming of God's Kingdom

From time immemorial, whenever the world is really burning, really suffering with sins and oppression, God has sent His Messengers to educate people in dharam. He has empowered a few good people with His Spirit, and through them has changed the whole world. God never becomes angry. When the world is suffering, He takes a few people and begins to build love in the world again.

The world has become so polluted; our minds have also become polluted. But when God's Love comes, it will be such a great wave that all the filth and corruption of the world will be swept away. God's Love is so powerful that nothing will remain in its way.

The time may finally be at hand again when That Power will come in the world and purify all of us. We should all join in prayer that God will bring the Light and Joy of His Kingdom on earth. We should all look to God and pray, *"Dear Lord, please bring Your happiness, Your love to the earth that exist in heaven. Take away the sorrows and the suffering in the world. Take away thoughts of rich and poor, high and low. Let us all sit together, eat together, live and work together in Your grace and harmony."*

Do not bewail the state of society. Change the state of your mind by sowing the seed of Nam. Do not waste a moment. As soon as you start meditating, reciting

Nam, and seeking God's Light within yourself, your life will change. As more and more people do so, the world will change.

God's Power has never left the world. From today, we should all follow God's teachings and anticipate that day when God transforms the world, and the Truth, which is now hidden, comes out and starts working among the people again. That day is upon us.

Gobind Sadan

"God's House Without Walls"

Rooted in the Sikh tradition and the teachings of its Gurus, Gobind Sadan, "God's House Without Walls" consists of self-supporting interfaith communities in India and elsewhere under the blessings of His Holiness Baba Virsa Singh. Gobind Sadan is dedicated to bringing people of all religions closer to God. People from all faiths—or no faith—find spiritual renewal, relief from stress, inner empowerment, and healing there. At Gobind Sadan, what some may consider miracles are everyday occurrences. Diseases are cured, business and personal problems, and even social conflicts are solved almost immediately through prayer at the various holy places. Babaji advocates a combination of hard work and meditation as modeled by volunteers from many different backgrounds who live and work together in this oasis on the outskirts of Delhi. An endless stream of people from all walks of life, from those in positions of power to common folk, continually seek Babaji's guidance and blessings.

Gobind Sadan's main "campus" includes the spiritual community with sites for prayer and meditation, "healing places," and Langar – the community kitchen. While guests are welcome, space is limited so it is advisable to write ahead to indicate your needs. info@gobindsadan.org.

Phone: 011-91-11-2680-1653; 2680-2251; Fax 2680-3398

www.gobindsadan.org
www.gobindsadan-info-ru

Sarawan Bodla – Babaji's village and place of enlightenment is a center of immense spiritual power and historic significance. One can sit under the same Beri Tree where Babaji used to meditate and heal people, and walk the soil of his youth.

Shiv Sadan – the main model farm developed from wastelands in the floodplains of the Holy River Ganges is based 300 kilometers from Delhi. Its crops provide food and income to run the langars and help those in need and also provide employment, employability training for thousands, and economic impact within the surrounding 50 kilometer radius. Those interested in issues of rural development, eradicating poverty, or pioneering agricultural methods are welcome to visit. At present facilities for overnight stay are extremely limited but seasonal day trips are possible.

GSI – Housed on Gobind Sadan's main campus the **Institute for Advanced Studies in Comparative Religions** consists of a research library, guest house, and auditorium for meetings and seminars. The library while small contains rare, often one of a kind religious and historical texts, and offers an ideal setting for research scholars. Scholars or students who wish to visit or come for a period in residence should contact us.

Gobind Sadan, USA – Babaji's first center outside of India is located in the heart of Central New York. Set on an old dairy farm and based on Gobind Sadan's model, it presently consists of a havan (sacred fire) and Gurdwara building. Plans for other sacred sites are in progress. For program and space consult the website under Gobind Sadan, USA. or contact gobindsadanusa@aol.com